Critical Thinking in Psychology

to accompany

Gerow
Psychology: An Introduction
Fifth Edition

prepared by

Shari Tishman
Harvard University
Project Zero

LONGMAN

An Imprint of Addison Wesley Longman, Inc

New York • Reading, Massachusetts •Menlo Park, California • Harlow, England
Don Mills, Ontario • Sydney • Mexico City • Madrid • Amsterdam

Critical Thinking in Psychology
to accompany *PSYCHOLOGY: AN INTRODUCTION, FIFTH EDITION*
by Josh Gerow

Copyright © 1997 Addison-Wesley Educational Publishers Inc.

ISBN: 0-673-97911-3

97 98 99 00 01 9 8 7 6 5 4 3 2

Introduction

This study supplement asks you to think critically about psychology. Broadly, its purpose is to challenge you to think about questions that can help you better understand and remember the material in *Psychology, An Introduction, Fifth Edition*. In the sections below, we offer a definition of critical thinking and say a few words about *how* critical thinking can help you better understand and remember the material in the text. But first, here is an overview of what you'll find in this supplement.

Overview

Critical Thinking and Psychology contains fifteen short sets of critical thinking questions. There are between six and ten questions in a set, and each set corresponds to a chapter in the textbook. As you'll discover when you open the text, most of the questions are keyed to a "before you go on" question.

Some of the questions will look familiar. The fifth edition of *Psychology, An Introduction,* includes some critical thinking questions in the textbook itself, and some of those questions are also included in this supplement.

There are several ways to use this supplement. You can work alone and answer the critical thinking questions in writing. You can work with a friend or in a small group of three or four students, and either answer the questions in writing or discuss them verbally. Any of these formats are effective. But working with a friend or in a group is especially recommended. The last section in this introduction provides guidelines for working in these formats, and for evaluating your own work.

You may be wondering whether critical thinking questions such as the ones located in this booklet will be on your course exams. They may or may not be: It is up to your instructor. However, thinking through these questions will almost certainly help you do a better job on the test, whether or not the test itself includes critical thinking questions.

What is Critical Thinking?

Critical thinking is active, high-level, reflective thinking that yields sound and creative products of thought — sound beliefs, sound ideas, reasonable decisions, innovative solutions, accurate explanations, reasonable hypotheses, and fruitful visions. This is a very broad definition, so it is reasonable to ask, "what *isn't* critical thinking?". Critical thinking doesn't include things like rote memorization, surface comprehension, passive learning, and unreflective thinking. Nor does it refer to basic literacies, although critical thinking can certainly play a role in their development.

Sometimes people use terms such as "thinking skills," "higher-order thinking" or "high-level thinking" to mean much the same thing as we mean here by the term "critical thinking." Although you may not call it by any of these names, you think critically all the time -- you're thinking critically when you think carefully about a decision, when you analyze the causes of a problem, when you construct a careful explanation, when you evaluate a theory or an argument, when you reason about the causes of an event, and when you build new ideas out of knowledge you already have.

How Can Critical Thinking Help Deepen Understanding and Make Retention More Effective?

It makes common sense that we tend to understand things better when we use them. For example, people who use hammers on a regular basis tend to understand them better than people who don't. People who regularly use the methods of scientific research in their work tend to understand them better than people who don't. As a general rule, this is true about the learning of any kind: The more you use and apply the information you are learning, the better you'll understand it.

Critical thinking is about the active use of information. Thinking critically with and about what you are learning means actively *using* the information you are studying to ask questions, to construct explanations and interpretations, to build and evaluate theories, and to make new connections and comparisons.

You may be thinking that it's all well and good that critical thinking helps deepen understanding, but what about memorization? After all, you have to *remember* much of the information you're learning in order to pass the test. So why should you worry about understanding? The answer is this: *Remembering and thinking are connected.* The pioneering American psychologist William James expressed it this way:

> ...the art of remembering is the art of *thinking*; ... when we wish to fix a thing either in our own mind or a pupil's, our conscious effort should not be so much to *impress* and *retain* it as to *connect* it with something else already there. The connecting *is* the thinking; and if we attend clearly to the connection; the connected thing will certainly be likely to remain within recall. (p. 87)[1]

Thinking critically with and about the information you are learning is the most powerful way to make the kinds of connections William James had in mind.

How To Use This Supplement

The questions in the supplement correspond to the chapters in the text. After you read a chapter, you can deepen your understanding of the information presented in it by asking yourself the corresponding critical thinking questions.

You can work alone while using the study supplement in the following way: ask yourself the questions, write down your responses, and evaluate your thinking according to the criteria described below.

Instead of working alone, you can use the supplement with another person or in a small group. In fact, working with others is recommended. To work with others, you can either write your responses to the questions individually after discussing them in a pair or group, or you can answer the questions entirely through collaborative group discussion.

Criteria For Evaluating your Work

Whether you work alone or with others, it's important to reflect on and evaluate your own thinking as part of the process of using this supplement. Here are three criteria to help you reflect on your thinking. Use these criteria as standards for guiding your thinking as you are working through the questions, and also as standards for evaluating your own and others' finished responses.

- *Reaching for Connections.* This concerns how well you push yourself to think beyond the obvious to find new ideas, new applications, and new connections. It concerns the extent to which you aim to make meaningful connections with the material you are studying and the extent to which you use what you are learning to adventure into new intellectual territory. In a sense, the most "subjective" of the evaluative criteria -- "reaching for connections" -- is about the spirit of adventure and willingness to take intellectual risks that you bring to the learning enterprise. It is an important criterion not because it yields right or wrong answers, but because it underlies and supports the active use of knowledge that is the hallmark of critical thinking and meaningful learning.

- *Quality of explanation* concerns the thoroughness, relevance, and accuracy of your explanations. For example, if you are constructing a causal explanation, your explanation should take into account obvious and hidden causes, and distinguish between causes and correlations. If you are constructing a descriptive explanation of a phenomenon, the explanation should take into account the key features of the phenomenon, and the purposes or functions that the features serve. If you are constructing a comparative explanation of two or more different views or theories, the explanation should take into account salient and defining features of the objects of comparison, and also demonstrate an understanding of the explanatory intent of the objects of comparison, i.e. an understanding of what phenomena the views or theories are trying to explain.

- *Quality of justification* concerns how well you provide reasons and evidence for your views, explanations, and hypotheses. Are your supporting reasons appropriate? Do they take into account available evidence? Do they take into account important possible objections? Do they demonstrate, when relevant, an understanding of multiple perspectives and points of view?

1. James, W. (1983). Talks to teachers on psychology. Cambridge, MA: Harvard University Press.

Chapter One
Psychology: What Psychologists Do

Can you think of any questions for which science would be an inappropriate technique to use?

What sort of cognitions or affects might be challenging for psychologists to operationally define? Why?

Descartes theorized that people were born with certain basic ideas already in their minds. Locke theorized that the mind started as a blank slate. Suppose you had unlimited resources at your disposal. What sort of experiment might shed light on either of these theories?

Structuralism and functionalism represent two very different ways of thinking about the nature of mental life. Can you think of other professions or areas of life which have similarly opposing perspectives?

Suppose John Watson and Sigmund Freud met by chance on a train. What do you think they might have talked about? On what issues would they agree and on what issues would they disagree?

Choose two or three of the five principles just discussed, and apply them to an experience in your own life. For example, suppose you are the kind of person who gets anxious before a test. Principle One states: "Our biological nature and psychological nurture interact to make us who we are." Principle Three states: "Our experience of the world may reflect something other than what is actually 'out there'." How might these principles apply to your feeling of anxiousness before a test?

You have a hypothesis: people who like sports have more friends than those who do not like sports. How would you conduct three different studies, one using naturalistic observation, one using surveys, and one using case histories to investigate your hypothesis. What would be the strengths and weaknesses of each method?

Think of a trick or technique you use to help you learn better (maybe it involves using a special pencil, eating a big breakfast, or assuming a certain posture). How would you design an experiment to test whether the usefulness of your technique is generalizable to other people?

Chapter Two
The Nervous Systems and Behavior

Think of another activating process you know about (e.g. internal combustion, photosynthesis). In what ways is this process like and unlike the process of a neuron firing?

Explain the following story in terms of the endocrine system:

Joe is 14 years old, and he's already 5'11" tall. Worried about his rapid growth, he had a bad night's sleep last night. His lack of sleep heightened his natural superstitiousness: as he was running to catch the school bus this morning, a black cat crossed in front of him, and Joe practically jumped out of his skin.

Can you think of a misconception or misunderstanding someone might have about how the spinal cord works?

Can you give an example not mentioned in the text of a bodily function that might be controlled by the medulla?

Choose any one of the structures just mentioned. What are two questions a research scientist might ask about how that structure affects specific human behaviors?

What kinds of conclusions about hemispheric specialization may be unwarranted? Why?

Chapter Three
Sensation and Perception

What examples could you provide to explain the differences between sensation and perception to people who confuse these two processes?

What are three reasons it might be important to understand the physical characteristics of light?

What evidence can you imagine that would be counter to this claim?

Is it possible to imagine an experience or experiment that would definitively prove that one or both of these theories is *wrong*?

Compare the senses of sight and sound to the chemical senses: What are their similarities? What are their differences?

What might be the consequences, positive and negative, of reducing pain?

Think about a time when you experienced an event differently than someone you were with. (e.g. a movie, a conversation, a date). Explain the differences in your experiences in terms of perceptual selectivity.

For what sorts of professions might it be particularly important to understand how stimuli are organized in perception?

Chapter 4
Varieties of Consciousness

Take a moment to focus on your own state of consciousness. In what ways does it fit James' features? Can you identify features of your present state of consciousness that aren't captured in James' list?

List three questions about the nature of consciousness. Be imaginative! Then, list three reasons why might be a challenge to study consciousness scientifically.

Choose one of the theories about REM just discussed. What sort of research experiment can you imagine that might test the theory? What kind of findings would count as evidence FOR the theory? What kinds of findings would count as evidence against it?

Of everything you just read about hypnosis, which idea stands out to you as the most provocative or interesting? Why?

You're probably familiar with the obvious consequences of the abuse of stimulant drugs. What might be some of the hidden consequences?

What reasons might people have for voluntarily altering consciousness? Are some reasons better than others? Why or why not?

Chapter 5
Learning

Can you think of two examples of classical conditioning in your own behavior?

Think again about one of the examples of classical conditioning in your own behavior you identified a few pages ago. Is your conditioned response generalized to other similar stimuli? What would constitute discrimination training for your conditioned response?

List three fears for which systematic desensitization might work well and might not work well. Explain the difference between these two lists.

Can you think of any risks that might be associated with systematic desensitization?

Suppose you wanted to understand classical conditioning much better than you do now. What are some steps you could take to develop your understanding further?

Identify two instances of operant conditioning in your own life.

Think again of one of the instances of operant conditioning in your own life you identified a few pages ago. How could you reconstruct the experience to include shaping, acquisition, extinction, and spontaneous recovery?

Suppose you wanted to teach your pet monkey to let himself in and out of the house by himself. How could you do it by using positive reinforcers? How could you do it by using negative reinforcers?

Is effectiveness an adequate justification for the use of punishers? Why or why not?

Suppose you are a teacher who is intrigued by the idea of latent learning and cognitive maps. How might you redesign your teaching technique to take advantage of these learning processes?

Some behaviors may be more effectively learned through modeling than others. What sort of learning might NOT effectively occur through exposure to models?

Chapter 6
Memory

What are three examples of your own sensory memory in the last two hours?

The idea of sensory memory is an attempt to explain the phenomenon of brief storage of large amounts of minimally processed information. Can you think of other plausible explanations?

Suppose you wanted to improve your memory. Identify three ways that knowing about the magical number 7 +/- 2 and "chunking" could be useful to you.

What sorts of factors might affect the reliability of eyewitness testimony?

List three ways in which you could consciously and systematically use elaborative rehearsal to do a better job of remembering the information in this textbook.

Suppose that the three subsystems of LTM are represented by three slightly overlapping circles. Can you identify paradigmatic cases of LTM in each subsystem (cases that fall near or in the center of each circle)? Can you identify ambiguous cases of LTM (cases that fall near or at the overlap of the circles)?

What questions can you raise about the effect of context on retrieval?

How can you make what you've learned about meaningfulness more meaningful to you?

Why do mnemonic devices work? Choose one of the mnemonic devices I've described and, based on what you've learned about memory, propose an explanation for why it works. Then, identify reasons for *and* against your explanation.

How would you design a study strategy for this course that took advantage of overlearning and distributed practice?

Chapter 7
Intelligence, Language, and Problem Solving

In what ways are these four conceptions of intelligence similar? Can you imagine a view of what counts as intelligent behavior that is very different than these four views?

Compare the Wechsler and Stanford-Binet intelligence scales. What are their similarities and differences?

What sorts of social factors might contribute to gender differences in IQ scores?

Suppose you were designing an intelligence test. What sorts of test items would you want to exclude, in order to avoid gender bias?

One question we haven't addressed is whether intelligence can be increased through learning, and, if so, through what kind of learning. What sort of research might you look for or conduct, in order to try to answer this question?

Think of three people you've known in your life who you think are mentally gifted. Does your "everyday" notion of mental giftedness (the one you used to identify the three people) match the definition of giftedness presented here? Would you argue for any adding to or deleting any of the six areas of giftedness listed here?

What are some features of language that you, personally, find particularly intriguing?

In what ways might the study of pragmatics inform professional practices (e.g. law, medicine, business)?

Think of a skill you've developed (e.g. bicycle riding, debating, rollerblading, cooking), and compare the learning of it to language acquisition. What are the similarities? The differences?

What kind of skill have you acquired that is most like language acquisition? Why?

What connections might there be between intelligence, and the ability to solve ill-defined problems?

Can you imagine a complex everyday problem for which you might use both algorithmic and heuristic strategies in working towards a solution?

What connections can you make between mental sets and functional fixedness, and the obstacles to memory retrieval discussed in the previous chapter?

I mentioned that there was virtually no correlation between creative problem solving and intelligence. Can you advance an argument for reconceiving intelligence to *include* creative problem solving ability?

Chapter 8
Human Development

How could we increase our understanding of the impact of the environment on prenatal development by examining the practices of other cultures?

How would you define "thinking" in a neonate? What evidence would you have to generate to demonstrate that neonates think?

Think about your experience observing younger siblings and other children. What behaviors have you observed that clearly characterize one of Piaget's four stages of cognitive development? Can you think of any behaviors you've observed that don't fit well within Piaget's four stages?

Compare Erikson's theory of psychosocial development with Kohlberg's theory of moral development. What do the two theories have on common? How do they differ?

List two questions about gender identity raised but not answered by the research discussed above.

Having been an adolescent, what do your own experiences tell you about the adolescent stage of development in terms of the "abnormal being normal"?

How might Kohlberg's theory of moral development apply to the adolescent years?. What kinds of moral challenges do you think might accompany adolescence?

Identify one of the statistics mentioned about adolescent sexuality that you found striking. What kinds of broad social or economic forces might contribute to the statistic you identified. What kinds of misinterpretations might the statistic provoke?

If there really is no such thing as a "mid-life crisis," why do so many people seem to act as if there were?

Think back on the thinking you did while reading this chapter: Identify one topic it discussed that seems fuzzy or unclear to you. What was unclear about it? What could you do to understand it better?

Chapter 9
Personality

Can you think of three mental events in the last twenty four hours of your own life that illustrate the three levels of consciousness?

Critics argue that several aspects of the psychoanalytic theory are "untestable". Identify one aspect of psychoanalytic theory that seems to you particularly *plausible*. Is it possible to devise an experiment to test it? Why or why not?

Imagine an individual who is honest and thoughtful. How would psychoanalytic theory explain this individual's personality? How would his or her personality be explained through behavioral-learning theory?

Consider the psychoanalytic, humanistic-phenomenological, and trait approaches to explaining personality development. Choose one of the approaches and use it to construct an interpretation of your own academic performance. For example, from the psychoanalytic perspective, in what ways might unconscious influences contribute to your academic performance? From the trait approach, how might the "big five" be used to describe your academic performance?

Suppose Freud was able to review the current research on personality and gender. Would he have cause to reconsider or revise some of his views? Why or why not?

List two things personality assessments *can't* reliably tell us about people.

Look over the glossary and choose one term that you find particularly intriguing, then brainstorm three questions about it.

Chapter 10
Motivation and Emotion

Do you find Maslow's theory intuitively appealing? Why or why not?

What are three possible pros and cons of using an incentive approach to motivate human behavior?

What are instructors really trying to do when they say they want to "motivate their students" to do as well as they can? Consider the motivational concepts of need, incentives, and balance in terms of the classroom: How might instructors use these concepts motivate students to learn better?

Think about your own experiences. Use the idea of internal and external cues to explain why you eat what you eat, when you eat.

Based on the research reported here, what sorts of unwarranted assumptions do people tend to make about homosexuality?

Describe three examples of human behavior, one of which is clearly motivated by nAch, one of which is clearly motivated by the need for power, and one of which is clearly motivated by the need for affiliation. Can you think of some examples of human behavior in which it is ambiguous which, or which combination of, these three motivations are at work?

Do you think that there is a list of basic emotions that is true for all people in all cultures? Why or why not?

Reflect for a moment on the thinking you did while reading this chapter. What ideas struck you as particularly interesting? What ideas puzzled or confused you? If you were to choose one idea reported in this Chapter to study more deeply, which would it be? Why?

Chapter 11
Psychology, Stress, and Physical Health

This is the second time I've mentioned the assumption that all behaviors are goal-directed. Can you think of any behaviors for which this might not be true?

How is it possible to reflect on all of the stressors in our lives and remain optimistic?

Do you see any general gender differences in the manner in which people you know deal with stressors in their lives. If so, how would you explain those differences? Can you think of two alternative explanations?

Think of a situation in which you or someone you know responded to a stressful situation in a positive way. Explain that response in terms of the adaptive behaviors just discussed.

Recall Freud's defense mechanism, in our last chapter. Where do these fit in our discussion of stressors, stress, and reactions to them?

Consider yourself. Can you easily be classified as either Type A or Type B? Why or why not?

alternative

To the extent that Type A or B behavior is learned, describe what kinds of environmental factors might influence the development of the behaviors.

What would be the consequences of simply passing a law banning the use, sale, possession of cigarettes in this country? Could passing such a law be justified? Why or why not?

Many argue that the incidence of AIDS would be reduced if more people practiced abstinence. What can you say for and against such an argument?

Chapter 12
The Psychological Disorders

Why do you think that someone who is willing to tell us about his or her physical illness (e.g. the gory details of a recent surgery), will probably be unwilling to share experiences with psychological disorders?

What kinds of cautions about your own thinking will you try to keep in mind as you read this chapter on psychological disorders?

Phobias are characterized as an intense, irrational fear. What is the difference, if any, between fear and anxiety?

Can you think of two alternative explanations for why the prognosis for OCD is currently not very good?

What connections can you make between personality disorders and the discussion of personality traits in Chapter nine?

Suppose there were a test available today that would tell you whether you would get Alzheimer's dementia when you became older, would you opt have the test? Under what conditions?

In what ways might mood affect how well you think and learn? What sort of experiment might shed light on this question?

What does the fact that schizophrenia occurs at about the same rate around the world suggest about its cause or etiology?

Think back on everything you've learned about psychological disorders in the chapter. List three big questions you have, either about the concept of psychological disorder in general, or about specific psychological disorders.

Chapter 13
Treatment and Therapy

The history of treatment reflects some misguided assumptions about the nature and causes of psychological disorders. What assumptions are embedded in our current views of psychological disorders? Are there any assumptions that warrant probing?

Suppose you were a major drug company who produced drugs for one of the three drug therapies just discussed. What sort of future research concerning this drug therapy would you see as promising?

Brainstorm three unusual alternatives to deinstitutionalization (be imaginative!). Then, choose one of your ideas and list reasons for and against it.

Which of the four features of Freudian psychoanalysis do you find most intriguing or most provocative. Why?

What do you consider to be one strength and one weakness of client-centered therapy, and gestalt therapy.

At some point during your school career, you have probably been exposed to some form of one or more of these behavior therapy techniques. Identify an occasion in which one these techniques was employed to manage or modify student behavior. Was the technique successful? Why or why not?

What are the fundamental differences between behavior therapy and cognitive techniques? What are some similarities?

In what ways did this section challenge and/or support any assumptions you previously had about psychotherapy?

Chapter 14
Social Psychology

Can you identify and affective, behavioral, and cognitive component in any of the attitudes you have?

Imagine that you want to change a friend's attitude about abortion (in either direction). How would you do so?

Think of an attribution you've made recently concerning why a friend or family member acted the way he or she did. Which of the attribution errors, if any, might you have made?

Can you explain your own interpersonal attraction to any of your friends in terms of the theories or factors presented above. Can you think of any counterexamples among your friendships -- instances where these factors don't seem to explain the attraction?

What is your view of the ethics of Milgram's research. Explain your reasons.

To what extent can you observe "bystander apathy" on your campus? For example, what percentage of the student body participates in campus elections?

How might social influence affect learning in groups? For example, recall an occasion when you were involved in a group project. In what ways, if at all, did the group influence your learning behaviors?

Chapter 15
Industrial/Organizational, Environmental,
and Sports Psychology

Consider your most recent job. Could you write a complete job analysis for that job — an analysis that takes into account both your perspective and that of your employer?

Consider some of the different psychological tests and assessments discussed in previous chapters. Which ones might be useful in gaining information about prospective employees? What sorts of issues or problems might be raised by certain tests?

In what ways might the factors that affect the motivation of workers be relevant to the motivation of students in school? In what ways might they not be relevant?

In what other areas of life might one find a complex relationship between satisfaction and productivity?

Recall examples from your own experience in which you felt your personal space or territory had been invaded. What did you notice about your own behavior or reactions? Can you think of instances when the behavior of others indicated you might have invaded their personal space?

One slogan of the environmentalist movement is to "think globally and act locally." What are the psychological implications of such a challenge?

Typically, mental imagery techniques are associated with athletic performances. In what ways might these sorts of techniques be applied to non-sporting performances like giving a speech, taking a test, or practicing the cello?